To Maria,

Robert Frost's verse depicts his ability to speak of great deeds and universal truths. His capacity to "see greatness in the familiar and simplicity in the grandiose" makes this volume a particularly appropriate gift for you.

We will miss you.

Gerry Day
Mary Bogh

June 1981

IN THE CLEARING BY ROBERT FROST

IN THE
CLEARING
BY
ROBERT
FROST

HOLT, RINEHART AND WINSTON

NEW YORK

First hardbound edition published in 1962
Fifteenth printing, 1979

First Holt paperback edition published in 1972
Fourth printing, 1979

Library of Congress Catalog Card Number: 62-11578

Note: "The Gift Outright" (page 31), which concludes "For John F. Kennedy His Inauguration," and which Mr. Frost read at the Inaugural ceremonies, January 20, 1961, in Washington, D.C., was first published in *A Witness Tree*, 1942.

ISBN Hardbound: 0-03-031010-5
ISBN Paperback: 0-03-086744-4

Printed in the United States of America

But God's own descent
Into flesh was meant
As a demonstration
That the supreme merit
Lay in risking spirit
In substantiation.
Spirit enters flesh
And for all it's worth
Charges into earth
In birth after birth
Ever fresh and fresh.
We may take the view
That its derring-do
Thought of in the large
Is one mighty charge
On our human part
Of the soul's ethereal
Into the material.

CONTENTS

IN THE CLEARING

"And wait to watch the water clear, I may."

Pod of the Milkweed

Calling all butterflies of every race
From source unknown but from no special place
They ever will return to all their lives,
Because unlike the bees they have no hives,
The milkweed brings up to my very door
The theme of wanton waste in peace and war
As it has never been to me before.
And so it seems a flower's coming out
That should if not be talked then sung about.
The countless wings that from the infinite
Make such a noiseless tumult over it
Do no doubt with their color compensate
For what the drab weed lacks of the ornate.
For drab it is its fondest must admit.
And yes, although it is a flower that flows
With milk and honey, it is bitter milk,
As anyone who ever broke its stem
And dared to taste the wound a little knows.
It tastes as if it might be opiate.
But whatsoever else it may secrete,
Its flowers' distilled honey is so sweet
It makes the butterflies intemperate.
There is no slumber in its juice for them.
One knocks another off from where he clings.
They knock the dyestuff off each other's wings —
With thirst on hunger to the point of lust.
They raise in their intemperance a cloud

Of mingled butterfly and flower dust
That hangs perceptibly above the scene.
In being sweet to these ephemerals
The sober weed has managed to contrive
In our three hundred days and sixty five
One day too sweet for beings to survive.
Many shall come away as struggle worn
And spent and dusted off of their regalia
To which at daybreak they were freshly born
As after one-of-them's proverbial failure
From having beaten all day long in vain
Against the wrong side of a window pane.

But waste was of the essence of the scheme.
And all the good they did for man or god
To all those flowers they passionately trod
Was leave as their posterity one pod
With an inheritance of restless dream.
He hangs on upside down with talon feet
In an inquisitive position odd
As any Guatemalan parakeet.
Something eludes him. Is it food to eat?
Or some dim secret of the good of waste?
He almost has it in his talon clutch.
Where have those flowers and butterflies all gone
That science may have staked the future on?
He seems to say the reason why so much
Should come to nothing must be fairly faced.*

*And shall be in due course.

14

Away!

Now I out walking
The world desert,
And my shoe and my stocking
Do me no hurt.

I leave behind
Good friends in town.
Let them get well-wined
And go lie down.

Don't think I leave
For the outer dark
Like Adam and Eve
Put out of the Park.

Forget the myth.
There is no one I
Am put out with
Or put out by.

Unless I'm wrong
I but obey
The urge of a song:
I'm — bound — away!

And I may return
If dissatisfied
With what I learn
From having died.

A Cabin in the Clearing

for Alfred Edwards

MIST

I don't believe the sleepers in this house
Know where they are.

SMOKE

They've been here long enough
To push the woods back from around the house
And part them in the middle with a path.

MIST

And still I doubt if they know where they are.
And I begin to fear they never will.
All they maintain the path for is the comfort
Of visiting with the equally bewildered.
Nearer in plight their neighbors are than distance.

SMOKE

I am the guardian wraith of starlit smoke
That leans out this and that way from their chimney.
I will not have their happiness despaired of.

MIST

No one — not I — would give them up for lost
Simply because they don't know where they are.
I am the damper counterpart of smoke

That gives off from a garden ground at night
But lifts no higher than a garden grows.
I cotton to their landscape. That's who I am.
I am no further from their fate than you are.

SMOKE

They must by now have learned the native tongue.
Why don't they ask the Red Man where they are?

MIST

They often do, and none the wiser for it.
So do they also ask philosophers
Who come to look in on them from the pulpit.
They will ask anyone there is to ask —
In the fond faith accumulated fact
Will of itself take fire and light the world up.
Learning has been a part of their religion.

SMOKE

If the day ever comes when they know who
They are, they may know better where they are.
But who they are is too much to believe —
Either for them or the onlooking world.
They are too sudden to be credible.

MIST

Listen, they murmur talking in the dark
On what should be their daylong theme continued.
Putting the lamp out has not put their thought out.

Let us pretend the dewdrops from the eaves
Are you and I eavesdropping on their unrest —
A mist and smoke eavesdropping on a haze —
And see if we can tell the bass from the soprano.

Than smoke and mist who better could appraise
The kindred spirit of an inner haze.

Closed for Good

They come not back with steed
And chariot to chide
My slowness with their speed
And scare me to one side.
They have found other scenes
For haste and other means.

They leave the road to me
To walk in saying naught
Perhaps but to a tree
Inaudibly in thought,
"From you the road receives
A priming coat of leaves.

"And soon for lack of sun,
The prospects are in white
It will be further done,
But with a coat so light
The shape of leaves will show
Beneath the spread of snow."

And so on into winter
Till even I have ceased
To come as a foot printer,
And only some slight beast
So mousy or so foxy
Shall print there as my proxy.

America Is Hard to See

Columbus may have worked the wind
A new and better way to Ind
And also proved the world a ball,
But how about the wherewithal?
Not just for scientific news
Had the Queen backed him to a cruise.

Remember he had made the test
Finding the East by sailing West.
But had he found it? Here he was
Without one trinket from Ormuz
To save the Queen from family censure
For her investment in his venture.

There had been something strangely wrong
With every coast he tried along.
He could imagine nothing barrener.
The trouble was with him the mariner.
He wasn't off a mere degree;
His reckoning was off a sea.

And to intensify the drama
Another mariner, Da Gama,
Came just then sailing into port
From the same general resort,
And with the gold in hand to show for
His claim it was another Ophir.

Had but Columbus known enough
He might have boldly made the bluff
That better than Da Gama's gold
He had been given to behold
The race's future trial place,
A fresh start for the human race.

He might have fooled Valladolid.
I was deceived by what he did.
If I had had my chance when young
I should have had Columbus sung
As a god who had given us
A more than Moses' exodus.

But all he did was spread the room
Of our enacting out the doom
Of being in each other's way,
And so put off the weary day
When we would have to put our mind
On how to crowd but still be kind.

For these none too apparent gains
He got no more than dungeon chains
And such small posthumous renown
(A country named for him, a town,
A holiday) as where he is
He may not recognize for his.

They say his flagship's unlaid ghost
Still probes and dents our rocky coast

With animus approaching hate,
And for not turning out a strait,
He has cursed every river mouth
From fifty North to fifty South.

Some day our navy, I predict,
Will take in tow this derelict
And lock him through Culebra Cut,
His eyes as good (or bad) as shut
To all the modern works of man
And all we call American.

America is hard to see.
Less partial witnesses than he
In book on book have testified
They could not see it from outside —
Or inside either for that matter.
We know the literary chatter.

Columbus, as I say, will miss
All he owes to the artifice
Of tractor-plow and motor-drill.
To naught but his own force of will,
Or at most some Andean quake,
Will he ascribe this lucky break.

High purpose makes the hero rude;
He will not stop for gratitude.
But let him show his haughty stern
To what was never his concern

Except as it denied him way
To fortune-hunting in Cathay.

He will be starting pretty late.
He'll find that Asiatic state
Is about tired of being looted
While having its beliefs disputed.
His can be no such easy raid
As Cortez on the Aztecs made.

One More Brevity

I opened the door so my last look
Should be taken outside a house and book.
Before I gave up seeing and slept
I said I would see how Sirius kept
His watch-dog eye on what remained
To be gone into if not explained.
But scarcely was my door ajar,
When past the leg I thrust for bar
Slipped in to be my problem guest,
Not a heavenly dog made manifest,
But an earthly dog of the carriage breed;
Who, having failed of the modern speed,
Now asked asylum — and I was stirred
To be the one so dog-preferred.
He dumped himself like a bag of bones,
He sighed himself a couple of groans,
And head to tail then firmly curled
Like swearing off on the traffic world.
I set him water, I set him food.
He rolled an eye with gratitude
(Or merely manners it may have been),
But never so much as lifted chin.
His hard tail loudly smacked the floor
As if beseeching me, "Please, no more,
I can't explain — tonight at least."
His brow was perceptibly trouble-creased.

So I spoke in terms of adoption thus:
"Gustie, old boy, Dalmatian Gus,
You're right, there's nothing to discuss.
Don't try to tell me what's on your mind,
The sorrow of having been left behind,
Or the sorrow of having run away.
All that can wait for the light of day.
Meanwhile feel obligation-free.
Nobody has to confide in me."
'Twas too one-sided a dialogue,
And I wasn't sure I was talking dog.
I broke off baffled. But all the same
In fancy, I ratified his name,
Gustie, Dalmatian Gus, that is,
And started shaping my life to his,
Finding him in his right supplies
And sharing his miles of exercise.

Next morning the minute I was about
He was at the door to be let out
With an air that said, "I have paid my call.
You mustn't feel hurt if now I'm all
For getting back somewhere or further on."
I opened the door and he was gone.
I was to taste in little the grief
That comes of dogs' lives being so brief,
Only a fraction of ours at most.
He might have been the dream of a ghost

In spite of the way his tail had smacked
My floor so hard and matter-of-fact.
And things have been going so strangely since
I wouldn't be too hard to convince,
I might even claim, he was Sirius
(Think of presuming to call him Gus)
The star itself, Heaven's greatest star,
Not a meteorite, but an avatar,
Who had made an overnight descent
To show by deeds he didn't resent
My having depended on him so long,
And yet done nothing about it in song.*
A symbol was all he could hope to convey,
An intimation, a shot of ray,
A meaning I was supposed to seek,
And finding, wasn't disposed to speak.

* But see "The Great Overdog" and "Choose Something
Like a Star," in which latter the star could hardly have
been a planet since fixity is of the essence of the piece.

Escapist — Never

He is no fugitive — escaped, escaping.
No one has seen him stumble looking back.
His fear is not behind him but beside him
On either hand to make his course perhaps
A crooked straightness yet no less a straightness.
He runs face forward. He is a pursuer.
He seeks a seeker who in his turn seeks
Another still, lost far into the distance.
Any who seek him seek in him the seeker.
His life is a pursuit of a pursuit forever.
It is the future that creates his present.
All is an interminable chain of longing.

For John F. Kennedy His Inauguration

GIFT OUTRIGHT OF
"THE GIFT OUTRIGHT"

With Some Preliminary History in Rhyme

Summoning artists to participate
In the august occasions of the state
Seems something artists ought to celebrate.
Today is for my cause a day of days.
And his be poetry's old-fashioned praise
Who was the first to think of such a thing.
This verse that in acknowledgment I bring
Goes back to the beginning of the end
Of what had been for centuries the trend;
A turning point in modern history.
Colonial had been the thing to be
As long as the great issue was to see
What country'd be the one to dominate
By character, by tongue, by native trait,
The new world Christopher Columbus found.
The French, the Spanish, and the Dutch were downed
And counted out. Heroic deeds were done.
Elizabeth the First and England won.
Now came on a new order of the ages
That in the Latin of our founding sages
(Is it not written on the dollar bill
We carry in our purse and pocket still?)

God nodded his approval of as good.
So much those heroes knew and understood,
I mean the great four, Washington,
John Adams, Jefferson, and Madison, —
So much they knew as consecrated seers
They must have seen ahead what now appears,
They would bring empires down about our ears
And by the example of our Declaration
Make everybody want to be a nation.
And this is no aristocratic joke
At the expense of negligible folk.
We see how seriously the races swarm
In their attempts at sovereignty and form.
They are our wards we think to some extent
For the time being and with their consent,
To teach them how Democracy is meant.
"New order of the ages" did we say?
If it looks none too orderly today,
'Tis a confusion it was ours to start
So in it have to take courageous part.
No one of honest feeling would approve
A ruler who pretended not to love
A turbulence he had the better of.
Everyone knows the glory of the twain
Who gave America the aeroplane
To ride the whirlwind and the hurricane.
Some poor fool has been saying in his heart
Glory is out of date in life and art.
Our venture in revolution and outlawry

Has justified itself in freedom's story
Right down to now in glory upon glory.
Come fresh from an election like the last,
The greatest vote a people ever cast,
So close yet sure to be abided by,
It is no miracle our mood is high.
Courage is in the air in bracing whiffs
Better than all the stalemate an's and ifs.
There was the book of profile tales declaring
For the emboldened politicians daring
To break with followers when in the wrong,
A healthy independence of the throng,
A democratic form of right divine
To rule first answerable to high design.
There is a call to life a little sterner,
And braver for the earner, learner, yearner.
Less criticism of the field and court
And more preoccupation with the sport.
It makes the prophet in us all presage
The glory of a next Augustan age
Of a power leading from its strength and pride,
Of young ambition eager to be tried,
Firm in our free beliefs without dismay,
In any game the nations want to play.
A golden age of poetry and power
Of which this noonday's the beginning hour.

"THE GIFT OUTRIGHT"

The land was ours before we were the land's.
She was our land more than a hundred years
Before we were her people. She was ours
In Massachusetts, in Virginia,
But we were England's, still colonials,
Possessing what we still were unpossessed by,
Possessed by what we now no more possessed.
Something we were withholding made us weak
Until we found out that it was ourselves
We were withholding from our land of living,
And forthwith found salvation in surrender.
Such as we were we gave ourselves outright
(The deed of gift was many deeds of war)
To the land vaguely realizing westward,
But still unstoried, artless, unenhanced,
Such as she was, such as she would become.

CLUSTER OF FAITH

Accidentally on Purpose

The Universe is but the Thing of things,
The things but balls all going round in rings.
Some of them mighty huge, some mighty tiny,
All of them radiant and mighty shiny.

They mean to tell us all was rolling blind
Till accidentally it hit on mind
In an albino monkey in a jungle
And even then it had to grope and bungle,

Till Darwin came to earth upon a year
To show the evolution how to steer.
They mean to tell us, though, the Omnibus
Had no real purpose till it got to us.

Never believe it. At the very worst
It must have had the purpose from the first
To produce purpose as the fitter bred:
We were just purpose coming to a head.

Whose purpose was it? His or Hers or Its?
Let's leave that to the scientific wits.
Grant me intention, purpose, and design —
That's near enough for me to the Divine.

And yet for all this help of head and brain
How happily instinctive we remain,
Our best guide upward further to the light,
Passionate preference such as love at sight.

A Never Naught Song

There was never naught,
There was always thought.
But when noticed first
It was fairly burst
Into having weight.
It was in a state
Of atomic One.
Matter was begun —
And in fact complete,
One and yet discrete
To conflict and pair.
Everything was there
Every single thing
Waiting was to bring,
Clear from hydrogen
All the way to men.
It is all the tree
It will ever be,
Bole and branch and root
Cunningly minute.
And this gist of all
Is so infra-small
As to blind our eyes
To its every guise
And so render nil

The whole Yggdrasil.
Out of coming-in
Into having been!
So the picture's caught
Almost next to naught
But the force of thought.

Version

Once there was an Archer
And there was a minute
When He shot a shaft
On a New Departure.
Then He must have laughed:
Comedy was in it.
For the game He hunted
Was the non-existence,
And His shaft got blunted
On its non-resistance.

A Concept Self-Conceived

The latest creed that has to be believed
And entered in our childish catechism
Is that the All's a concept self-conceived,
Which is no more than good old Pantheism.

Great is the reassurance of recall.
Why go on further with confusing voice
To say God's either All or over all?
The rule is, never give a child a choice.

Forgive, O Lord, my little jokes on Thee
And I'll forgive Thy great big one on me.

Kitty Hawk

Back there in 1953 with the Huntington Cairnses

(A Skylark for Them in Three-Beat Phrases)

PART ONE

PORTENTS, PRESENTIMENTS,

AND PREMONITIONS

Kitty Hawk, O Kitty,
There was once a song,
Who knows but a great
Emblematic ditty,
I might well have sung
When I came here young
Out and down along
Past Elizabeth City
Sixty years ago.
I was, to be sure,
Out of sorts with Fate,
Wandering to and fro
In the earth alone,
You might think too poor-
Spirited to care
Who I was or where
I was being blown
Faster than my tread —
Like the crumpled, better
Left-unwritten letter

41

I had read and thrown.
Oh, but not to boast,
Ever since Nag's Head
Had my heart been great,
Not to claim elate,
With a need the gale
Filled me with to shout
Summary riposte
To the dreary wail
There's no knowing what
Love is all about.
Poets know a lot.
Never did I fail
Of an answer back
To the zodiac
When in heartless chorus
Aries and Taurus,
Gemini and Cancer
Mocked me for an answer.
It was on my tongue
To have up and sung
The initial flight
I can see now might —
Should have been my own —
Into the unknown,
Into the sublime
Off these sands of Time
Time had seen amass
From his hourglass.

Once I told the Master,
Later when we met,
I'd been here one night
As a young Alastor
When the scene was set
For some kind of flight
Long before he flew it.
Just supposing I —
I had beat him to it.
What did men mean by
THE original?
Why was it so very,
Very necessary
To be first of all?
How about the lie
That he wasn't first?
I was glad he laughed.
There was such a lie
Money and maneuver
Fostered over long
Until Herbert Hoover
Raised this tower shaft
To undo the wrong.
Of all crimes the worst
Is to steal the glory
From the great and brave,
Even more accursed
Than to rob the grave.
But the sorry story

Has been long redressed.
And as for my jest
I had any claim
To the runway's fame
Had I only sung,
That is all my tongue.
I can't make it seem
More than that my theme
Might have been a dream
Of dark Hatteras
Or sad Roanoke,
One more fond alas
For the seed of folk
Sowed in vain by Raleigh,
Raleigh of the cloak,
And some other folly.

Getting too befriended,
As so often, ended
Any melancholy
Götterdämmerung
That I might have sung.
I fell in among
Some kind of committee
From Elizabeth City,
Each and every one
Loaded with a gun
Or a demijohn.
(Need a body ask

If it was a flask?)
Out to kill a duck
Or perhaps a swan
Over Currituck.
This was not their day
Anything to slay
Unless one another.
But their lack of luck
Made them no less gay
No, nor less polite.
They included me
Like a little brother
In their revelry —
All concern to take
Care my innocence
Should at all events
Tenderly be kept
For good gracious' sake.
And if they were gentle
They were sentimental.
One drank to his mother
While another wept.
Something made it sad
For me to break loose
From the need they had
To make themselves glad
They were of no use.
Manners made it hard,
But that night I stole

Off on the unbounded
Beaches where the whole
Of the Atlantic pounded.
There I next fell in
With a lone coast guard
On midnight patrol,
Who as of a sect
Asked about my soul
And where-all I'd been.
Apropos of sin,
Did I recollect
How the wreckers wrecked
Theodosia Burr
Off this very shore?
'Twas to punish her,
But her father more —
We don't know what for:
There was no confession.
Things they think she wore
Still sometimes occur
In someone's possession
Here at Kitty Hawk.
We can have no notion
Of the strange devotion
Burr had for his daughter:
He was too devoted.
So it was in talk
We prolonged the walk,
On one side the ocean,

And on one a water
Of the inner sound;
"And the moon was full,"
As the poet said
And I aptly quoted.
And its being full
And right overhead,
Small but strong and round,
By its tidal pull
Made all being full.
Kitty Hawk, O Kitty,
Here it was again
In the selfsame day,
I at odds with men
Came upon their pity,
Equally profound
For a son astray
And a daughter drowned.

PART TWO

When the chance went by
For my Muse to fly
From this Runway Beach
As a figure of speech
In a flight of words,
Little I imagined
Men would treat this sky
Some day to a pageant

Like a thousand birds.
Neither you nor I
Ever thought to fly.
Oh, but fly we did,
Literally fly.
That's because though mere
Lilliputians we're
What Catullus called
Somewhat (aliquid).
Mind you, we are mind.
We are not the kind
To stay too confined.
After having crawled
Round the place on foot
And done yeoman share
Of just staying put,
We arose from there
And we scaled a plane
So the stilly air
Almost pulled our hair
Like a hurricane.

Then I saw it all.

Pulpiteers will censure
Our instinctive venture
Into what they call
The material
When we took that fall

From the apple tree.
But God's own descent
Into flesh was meant
As a demonstration
That the supreme merit
Lay in risking spirit
In substantiation.
Westerners inherit
A design for living
Deeper into matter —
Not without due patter
Of a great misgiving.
All the science zest
To materialize
By on-penetration
Into earth and skies
(Don't forget the latter
Is but further matter)
Has been West Northwest.
If it was not wise,
Tell me why the East
Seemingly has ceased
From its long stagnation
In mere meditation.
What is all the fuss
To catch up with us?
Can it be to flatter
Us with emulation?

Spirit enters flesh
And for all it's worth
Charges into earth
In birth after birth
Ever fresh and fresh.
We may take the view
That its derring-do
Thought of in the large
Was one mighty charge
On our human part
Of the soul's ethereal
Into the material.
In a running start
As it were from scratch
On a certain slab
Of (we'll say) basalt
In or near Moab
With intent to vault
In a vaulting match,
Never mind with whom —
(No one, I presume,
But ourselves — mankind,
In a love and hate
Rivalry combined.)
'Twas a radio
Voice that said, "Get set
In the alphabet,
That is A B C,
Which some day should be

Rhymed with 1 2 3
On a college gate."
Then the radio
Region voice said, "Go,
Go you on to know
More than you can sing.
Have no hallowing fears
Anything's forbidden
Just because it's hidden.
Trespass and encroach
On successive spheres
Without self-reproach."
Then for years and years
And for miles and miles
'Cross the Aegean Isles,
Athens Rome France Britain,
Always West Northwest,
As have I not written,
Till the so-long kept
Purpose was expressed
In the leap we leapt.
And the radio
Cried, "The Leap — The Leap!"
It belonged to US,
Not our friends the Russ,
To have run the event
To its full extent
And have won the crown,
Or let's say the cup,

On which with a date
Is the inscription though,
"Nothing can go up
But it must come down."
Earth is still our fate.
The uplifted sight
We enjoyed at night
When instead of sheep
We were counting stars,
Not to go to sleep,
But to stay awake
For good gracious' sake,
Naming stars to boot
To avoid mistake,
Jupiter and Mars,
Just like Pullman cars,
'Twas no vain pursuit.
Some have preached and taught
All there was to thought
Was to master Nature
By some nomenclature.
But if not a law
'Twas an end foregone
Anything we saw
And thus fastened on
With an epithet
We would see to yet —
We would want to touch
Not to mention clutch.

TALK ALOFT

Someone says the Lord
Says our reaching toward
Is its own reward.
One would like to know
Where God says it though.

We don't like that much.

Let's see where we are.
What's that sulphur blur
Off there in the fog?
Go consult the log.
It's some kind of town,
But it's not New York.
We're not very far
Out from where we were.
It's still Kitty Hawk.

We'd have got as far
Even at a walk.

Don't you crash me down.
Though our kiting ships
Prove but flying chips
From the science shop
And when motors stop
They may have to drop
Short of anywhere,

Though our leap in air
Prove as vain a hop
As the hop from grass
Of a grasshopper,
Don't discount our powers;
We have made a pass
At the infinite,
Made it, as it were,
Rationally ours,
To the most remote
Swirl of neon-lit
Particle afloat.
Ours was to reclaim
What had long been faced
As a fact of waste
And was waste in name.

That's how we became
Though an earth so small,
Justly known to fame
As the Capital
Of the universe.
We make no pretension
Of projecting ray
We can call our own
From this ball of stone,
None I don't reject
As too new to mention.
All we do's reflect

From our rocks, and yes,
From our brains no less.
And the better part
Is the ray we dart
From this head and heart,
The *mens animi.*

Till we came to be
There was not a trace
Of a thinking race
Anywhere in space.
We know of no world
Being whirled and whirled
Round and round the rink
Of a single sun
(So as not to sink),
Not a single one
That has thought to think.

THE HOLINESS
OF WHOLENESS

Pilot, though at best your
Flight is but a gesture,
And your rise and swoop,
But a loop the loop,
Lands on someone hard
In his own backyard
From no higher heaven
Than a bolt of levin,

I don't say retard.
Keep on elevating.
But while meditating
What we can't or can
Let's keep starring man
In the royal role.
It will not be his
Ever to create
One least germ or coal.
Those two things we can't.
But the comfort is
In the covenant
We may get control
If not of the whole
Of at least some part
Where not too immense,
So by craft or art
We can give the part
Wholeness in a sense.
The becoming fear
That becomes us best
Is lest habit ridden
In the kitchen midden
Of our dump of earning
And our dump of learning
We come nowhere near
Getting thought expressed.

THE MIXTURE
MECHANIC

This wide flight we wave
At the stars or moon
Means that we approve
Of them on the move.
Ours is to behave
Like a kitchen spoon
Of a size Titanic
To keep all things stirred
In a blend mechanic
Saying That's the tune,
That's the pretty kettle!
Matter mustn't curd,
Separate and settle.
Action is the word.

Nature's never quite
Sure she hasn't erred
In her vague design
Till on some fine night
We two come in flight
Like a king and queen
And by right divine,
Waving scepter-baton,
Undertake to tell her
What in being stellar
She's supposed to mean.

God of the machine,
Peregrine machine,
Some still think is Satan,
Unto you the thanks
For this token flight,
Thanks to you and thanks
To the brothers Wright
Once considered cranks
Like Darius Green
In their home town, Dayton.

Auspex

Once in a California Sierra
I was swooped down upon when I was small
And measured, but not taken after all
By a great eagle bird in all its terror.

Such auspices are very hard to read.
My parents when I ran to them averred
I was rejected by the royal bird
As one who would not make a Ganymede.

Not find a barkeep unto Jove in me?
I have remained resentful to this day
When any but myself presumed to say
That there was anything I couldn't be.

The Draft Horse

With a lantern that wouldn't burn
In too frail a buggy we drove
Behind too heavy a horse
Through a pitch-dark limitless grove.

And a man came out of the trees
And took our horse by the head
And reaching back to his ribs
Deliberately stabbed him dead.

The ponderous beast went down
With a crack of a broken shaft.
And the night drew through the trees
In one long invidious draft.

The most unquestioning pair
That ever accepted fate
And the least disposed to ascribe
Any more than we had to to hate,

We assumed that the man himself
Or someone he had to obey
Wanted us to get down
And walk the rest of the way.

Ends

Loud talk in the overlighted house
That made us stumble past.
Oh, there had once been night the first,
But this was night the last.

Of all the things he might have said,
Sincere or insincere,
He never said she wasn't young,
And hadn't been his dear.

Oh, some as soon would throw it all
As throw a part away.
And some will say all sorts of things,
But some mean what they say.

Peril of Hope

It is right in there
Betwixt and between
The orchard bare
And the orchard green,

When the orchard's right
In a flowery burst
Of pink and white,
That we fear the worst.

For there's not a clime
But at any cost
Will take that time
For a night of frost.

Questioning Faces

The winter owl banked just in time to pass
And save herself from breaking window glass.
And her wings straining suddenly aspread
Caught color from the last of evening red
In a display of underdown and quill
To glassed-in children at the window sill.

Does No One at All
Ever Feel This Way in the Least?

O ocean sea for all your being vast,
Your separation of us from the Old
That should have made the New World newly great
Would only disappoint us at the last
If it should not do anything foretold
To make us different in a single trait.

This though we took the Indian name for maize
And changed it to the English name for wheat.
It seemed to comfort us to call it corn.
And so with homesickness in many ways
We sought however crudely to defeat
Our chance of being people newly born.

And now, O sea, you're lost by aeroplane.
Our sailors ride a bullet for a boat.
Our coverage of distance is so facile
It makes us to have had a sea in vain.
Our moat around us is no more a moat,
Our continent no more a moated castle.

Grind shells, O futile sea, grind empty shells
For all the use you are along the strand.
I cannot hold you innocent of fault.
Spring water in our mountain bosom swells

To pour fresh rivers on you from the land.
Till you have lost the savor of your salt.*

I pick a dead shell up from where the kelp
Lies in a windrow, brittle dry and black,
And holding it far forward for a symbol
I cry "Do work for women — all the help
I ask of you. Grind this I throw you back
Into a lady's finger ring or thimble."

The ocean had been spoken to before.†
But if it had no thought of paying heed
To taunt of mine I knew a place to go
Where I need listen to its rote no more,
Nor taste its salt, nor smell its fish and weed,
Nor be reminded of them in a blow —

So far inland the very name of ocean
Goes mentionless except in baby-school
When teacher's own experiences fail her
And she can only give the class a notion
Of what it is by calling it a pool
And telling them how Sinbad was a sailor.

---

*At this writing it seems pretty well accepted that
any rivers added can only make the sea saltier.

†By King Canute and Lord Byron among others.

The Bad Island — Easter

(Perhaps so called because it may have risen once)

That primitive head
So ambitiously vast
Yet so rude in its art
Is as easily read
For the woes of the past
As a clinical chart.
For one thing alone,
The success of the lip
So scornfully curled
Has that tonnage of stone
Been brought in a ship
Half way round the world.

They were days on that stone.
They gave it the wedge
Till it flaked from the ledge.
Then they gave it a face.
Then with tackle unknown
They stood it in place
On a cliff for a throne.
They gave it a face
Of what was it? Scorn
Of themselves as a race
For having been born?
And then having first
Been cajoled and coerced

Into being be-ruled?
By what stratagem
Was their cynical throng
So cozened and fooled
And jollied along?
Were they told they were free
And persuaded to see
Something in it for them?
Well they flourished and waxed
By executive guile,
By fraud and by force,
Or so for a while;
Until overtaxed
In nerve and resource
They started to wane.
They emptied the aisle
Except for a few
That can but be described
As a vile residue,
And a garrulous too.
They were punished and bribed;
All was in vain,
Nothing would do.
Some mistake had been made
No book can explain,
Some change in the law
That nobody saw
Except as a gain.
But one thing is sure

Whatever kultur
They were made to parade,
What heights of altrur-
ian thought to attain,
Not a trace of it's left
But the gospel of sharing,
And that has decayed
Into a belief
In being a thief
And persisting in theft
With cynical daring.

Our Doom to Bloom

"Shine, perishing republic."

Cumaean Sibyl, charming Ogress,
What are the simple facts of Progress
That I may trade on with reliance
In consultation with my clients?
The Sibyl said, "Go back to Rome
And tell your clientele at home
That if it's not a mere illusion
All there is to it is diffusion —
Of coats, oats, votes, to all mankind.
In the Surviving Book we find
That liberal, or conservative,
The state's one function is to give.
The bud must bloom till blowsy blown
Its petals loosen and are strown;
And that's a fate it can't evade
Unless 'twould rather wilt than fade."

The Objection to Being Stepped On

At the end of the row
I stepped on the toe
Of an unemployed hoe.
It rose in offence
And struck me a blow
In the seat of my sense.
It wasn't to blame
But I called it a name.
And I must say it dealt
Me a blow that I felt
Like malice prepense.
You may call me a fool,
But *was* there a rule
The weapon should be
Turned into a tool?
And what do we see?
The first tool I step on
Turned into a weapon.

A-Wishing Well

A poet would a-wishing go,
And he wished love were thus and so.
"If but it were" he said, said he,
"And one thing more that may not be,
This world were good enough for me."
I quote him with respect verbatim.
Some quaint dissatisfaction ate him.
I would give anything to learn
The one thing more of his concern.
But listen to me register
The one thing more I wish there were.
As a confirmed astronomer
I'm always for a better sky.
(I don't care how the world gets by.)
I'm tempted to let go restraint
Like splashing phosphorescent paint,
And fill the sky as full of moons
As circus day of toy balloons.
That ought to make the Sunday Press.
But that's not like me. On much less
And much much easier to get
From childhood has my heart been set.
Some planets, the unblinking four,
Are seen to juggle moons galore.
A lot would be a lot of fun.
But all I ask's an extra one.
Let's get my incantation right:

"I wish I may I wish I might"
Give earth another satellite.
Where would we get another? Come,
Don't you know where new moons are from?
When clever people ask me where
I get a poem, I despair.
I'm apt to tell them in New York
I think I get it via stork
From some extinct old chimney pot.
Believe the Arcadians or not,
They claim they recollect the morn
When unto Earth her first was born.
It cost the Earth as fierce a pang
As Keats (or was it Milton?) sang
It cost her for Enormous Caf.
It came near splitting her in half.
'Twas torn from her Pacific side.
All the sea water in one tide
And all the air rushed to the spot.
Believe the Arcadians or not,
They saved themselves by hanging on
To a plant called the silphion,
Which has for its great attribute
It can't be pulled up by the root.
Men's legs and bodies in the gale
Streamed out like pennants swallow-tail.
Most of them let go and were gone.
But there was this phenomenon:
Some of them gave way at the wrist

Before they gave way at the fist.
In branches of the silphion
Is sometimes found a skeleton
Of desperately clutching hand
Science has failed to understand.
One has been lately all the talk
In the museum of Antioch.
That's how it was from the Pacific.
It needn't be quite so terrific
To get another from the Atlantic.
It needn't be quite so gigantic
As coming from a lesser ocean.
Good liberals will object my notion
Is too hard on the human race.
That's something I'm prepared to face.
It merely would entail the purge
That the just pausing Demiurge
Asks of himself once in so often
So the firm firmament won't soften.
I am assured at any rate
Man's practically inexterminate.
Someday I must go into that.
There's always been an Ararat
Where someone someone else begat
To start the world all over at.

How Hard It Is to Keep from Being King
When It's in You and in the Situation

The King said to his son: "Enough of this!
The Kingdom's yours to finish as you please.
I'm getting out tonight. Here, take the crown."

But the Prince drew away his hand in time
To avoid what he wasn't sure he wanted.
So the crown fell and the crown jewels scattered.
And the Prince answered, picking up the pieces,
"Sire, I've been looking on and I don't like
The looks of empire here. I'm leaving with you."

So the two making good their abdication
Fled from the palace in the guise of men.
But they had not walked far into the night
Before they sat down weary on a bank
Of dusty weeds to take a drink of stars.
And eycing one he only wished were his,
Rigel, Bellatrix, or else Betelgeuse,
The ex-King said, "Yon star's indifference
Fills me with fear I'll be left to my fate:
I needn't think I have escaped my duty,
For hard it is to keep from being King
When it's in you and in the situation.
Witness how hard it was for Julius Caesar.
He couldn't keep himself from being King.

He had to be stopped by the sword of Brutus.
Only less hard was it for Washington.
My crown shall overtake me, you will see,
It will come rolling after us like a hoop."

"Let's not get superstitious, Sire," the Prince said.
"We should have brought the crown along to pawn."
"You're right," the ex-King said, "we'll need some money.
How would it be for you to take your father–
To the slave auction in some market place
And sell him into slavery? My price
Should be enough to set you up in business –
Or making verse if that is what you're bent on.
Don't let your father tell you what to be."

The ex-King stood up in the market place
And tried to look ten thousand dollars' worth.
To the first buyer coming by who asked
What good he was he boldly said, "I'll tell you:
I know the *Quint*essence of many things.
I know the *Quint*essence of food, I know
The *Quint*essence of jewels, and I know
The *Quint*essence of horses, men, and women."

The eunuch laughed: "Well, that's a lot to know.
And here's a lot of money. Who's the taker?
This larrikin? All right. You come along.
You're off to Xanadu to help the cook.
I'll try you in the kitchen first on food

Since you put food first in your repertory.
It seems you call quint*ess*ence *quint*essence."

"I'm a Rhodes scholar — that's the reason why.
I was at college in the Isle of Rhodes."

The slave served his novitiate dish-washing.
He got his first chance to prepare a meal
One day when the chief cook was sick at heart.
(The cook was temperamental like the King)
And the meal made the banqueters exclaim
And the Great King inquire whose work it was.

"A man's out there who claims he knows the secret,
Not of food only but of everything,
Jewels and horses, women, wine, and song."
The King said grandly, "Even as we are fed
See that our slave is also. He's in favor.
Take notice, Haman, he's in favor with us."

There came to court a merchant selling pearls,
A smaller pearl he asked a thousand for,
A larger one he asked five hundred for.
The King sat favoring one pearl for its bigness,
And then the other for its costliness
(He seems to have felt limited to one),
Till the ambassadors from Punt or somewhere
Shuffled their feet as if to hint respectfully,
"The choice is not between two pearls, O King,

But between peace and war as we conceive it.
We are impatient for your royal answer."
No estimating how far the entente
Might have deteriorated had not someone
Thought of the kitchen slave and had him in
To put an end to the King's vacillation.

And the slave said, "The small one's worth the price,
But the big one is worthless. Break it open.
My head for it — you'll find the big one hollow.
Permit me" — and he crushed it under his heel
And showed them it contained a live teredo.

"But tell us how you knew," Darius cried.

"Oh, from my knowledge of its *quint*essence.
I told you I knew the quintessence of jewels.
But anybody could have guessed in this case,
From the pearl's having its own native warmth,
Like flesh, there must be something living in it."

"Feed him another feast of recognition."

And so it went with triumph after triumph
Till on a day the King, being sick at heart
(The King was temperamental like his cook,
But nobody had noticed the connection),
Sent for the ex-King in a private matter.
"You say you know the inwardness of men
As well as of your hundred other things.

Dare to speak out and tell me about myself.
What ails me? Tell me. Why am I unhappy?"

"You're not where you belong. You're not a King
Of royal blood. Your father was a cook."

"You die for that."
                              "No, you go ask your mother."

His mother didn't like the way he put it,
"But yes," she said, "some day I'll tell you, dear.
You have a right to know your pedigree.
You're well descended on your mother's side,
Which is unusual. So many kings
Have married beggar maids from off the streets.
Your mother's folks —"

                              He stayed to hear no more,
But hastened back to reassure his slave
That if he had him slain it wouldn't be
For having lied but having told the truth.
"At least you ought to die for wizardry.
But let me into it and I will spare you.
How did you know the secret of my birth?"

"If you had been a king of royal blood,
You'd have rewarded me for all I've done
By making me your minister-vizier,
Or giving me a nobleman's estate.
But all you thought of giving me was food.

I picked you out a horse called Safety Third
By Safety Second out of Safety First,
Guaranteed to come safely off with you
From all the fights you had a mind to lose.
You could lose battles, you could lose whole wars,
You could lose Asia, Africa, and Europe,
No one could get you: you would come through smiling.
You lost your army at Mosul. What happened?
You came companionless, but you came home.
Is it not true? And what was my reward?
This time an all-night banquet, to be sure,
But still food, food. Your one idea was food.
None but a cook's son could be so food-minded.
I knew your father must have been a cook.
I'll bet you anything that's all as King
You think of for your people — feeding them."

But the King said, "Haven't I read somewhere
There is no act more kingly than to give?"

"Yes, but give character and not just food.
A King must give his people character."

"They can't have character unless they're fed."

"You're hopeless," said the slave.

                    "I guess I am;
I am abject before you," said Darius.

"You know so much, go on, instruct me further.
Tell me some rule for ruling people wisely,
In case I should decide to reign some more.
How shall I give a people character?"

"Make them as happy as is good for them.
But that's a hard one, for I have to add:
Not without consultation with their wishes;
Which is the crevice that lets Progress in.
If we could only stop the Progress somewhere,
At a good point for pliant permanence,
Where Madison attempted to arrest it.
But no, a woman has to be her age,
A nation has to take its natural course
Of Progress round and round in circles
From King to Mob to King to Mob to King
Until the eddy of it eddies out."

"So much for Progress," said Darius meekly.
"Another word that bothers me is Freedom.
You're good at maxims. Say me one on Freedom.
What has it got to do with character?
My satrap Tissaphernes has no end
Of trouble with it in his Grecian cities
Along the Aegean coast. That's all they talk of."

"Behold my son in rags here with his lyre,"
The ex-King said. "We're in this thing together.
He is the one who took the money for me

When I was sold — and small reproach to him.
He's a good boy. 'Twas at my instigation.
I looked on it as a Carnegie grant
For him to make a poet of himself on
If such a thing is possible with money.
Unluckily it wasn't money enough
To be a test. It didn't last him out.
And he may have to turn to something else
To earn a living. I don't interfere.
I want him to be anything he has to.
He has been begging through the Seven Cities
Where Homer begged. He'll tell you about Freedom.
He writes free verse, I'm told, and he is thought
To be the author of the Seven Freedoms,
Free Will, Trade, Verse, Thought, Love, Speech, Coinage.
(You ought to see the coins done in Cos.)
His name is Omar. I as a Rhodes Scholar
Pronounce it Homer with a Cockney rough.
Freedom is slavery some poets tell us.
Enslave yourself to the right leader's truth,
Christ's or Karl Marx', and it will set you free.
Don't listen to their play of paradoxes.
The only certain freedom's in departure.
My son and I have tasted it and know.
We feel it in the moment we depart
As fly the atomic smithereens to nothing.
The problem for the King is just how strict
The lack of liberty, the squeeze of law
And discipline should be in school and state

To insure a jet departure of our going
Like a pip shot from 'twixt our pinching fingers."

"All this facility disheartens me.
Pardon my interruption; I'm unhappy.
I guess I'll have the headsman execute me
And press your father into being King."

"Don't let him fool you: he's a King already.
But though almost all-wise, he makes mistakes.
I'm not a free-verse singer. He was wrong there.
I claim to be no better than I am.
I write real verse in numbers, as they say.
I'm talking not free verse but blank verse now.
Regular verse springs from the strain of rhythm
Upon a metre, strict or loose iambic.
From that strain comes the expression *strains of music*.
The tune is not that metre, not that rhythm,
But a resultant that arises from them.
Tell them Iamb, Jehovah said, and meant it.
Free verse leaves out the metre and makes up
For the deficiency by church intoning.
Free verse so called is really cherished prose,
Prose made of, given an air by church intoning.
It has its beauty, only I don't write it.
And possibly my not writing it should stop me
From holding forth on Freedom like a Whitman —
A Sandburg. But permit me in conclusion:
Tell Tissaphernes not to mind the Greeks.

The freedom they seek is by politics,
Forever voting and haranguing for it.
The reason artists show so little interest
In public freedom is because the freedom
They've come to feel the need of is a kind
No one can give them — they can scarce attain —
The freedom of their own material;
So, never at a loss in simile,
They can command the exact affinity
Of anything they are confronted with.
This perfect moment of unbafflement,
When no man's name and no noun's adjective
But summons out of nowhere like a jinni.
We know not what we owe this moment to.
It may be wine, but much more likely love —
Possibly just well-being in the body,
Or respite from the thought of rivalry.
It's what my father must mean by departure,
Freedom to flash off into wild connections.
Once to have known it nothing else will do.
Our days all pass awaiting its return.
You must have read the famous valentine
Pericles sent Aspasia in absentia:

For God himself the height of feeling free
Must have been his success in simile
When at sight of you he thought of me.

Let's see, where are we? Oh, we're in transition,
Changing an old King for another old one.

What an exciting age it is we live in —
With all this talk about the hope of youth
And nothing made of youth. Consider me,
How totally ignored I seem to be.
No one is nominating me for King.
The headsman has Darius by the belt
To lead him off the Asiatic way
Into oblivion without a lawyer.
But that is as Darius seems to want it.
No fathoming the Asiatic mind.
And father's in for what we ran away from.
And superstition wins. He blames the stars,
Aldebaran, Capella, Sirius,
(As I remember they were summer stars
The night we ran away from Ctesiphon)
For looking on and not participating.
(Why are we so resentful of detachment?)
But don't tell me it wasn't his display
Of more than royal attributes betrayed him.
How hard it is to keep from being king
When it's in you and in the situation.
And that is half the trouble with the world
(Or more than half I'm half inclined to say)."

Lines Written in Dejection

on the Eve of Great Success

I once had a cow that jumped over the moon,
Not on to the moon but over.
I don't know what made her so lunar a loon;
All she'd been having was clover.

That was back in the days of my godmother Goose.
But though we are goosier now,
And all tanked up with mineral juice,
We haven't caught up with my cow.

POSTSCRIPT

But if over the moon I had wanted to go
And had caught my cow by the tail,
I'll bet she'd have made a melodious low
And put her foot in the pail;

Than which there is no indignity worse.
A cow did that once to a fellow
Who rose from the milking stool with a curse
And cried, "I'll larn you to bellow."

He couldn't lay hands on a pitchfork to hit her
Or give her a stab of the tine,
So he leapt on her hairy back and bit her
Clear into her marrow spine.

No doubt she would have preferred the fork.
She let out a howl of rage
That was heard as far away as New York
And made the papers' front page.

He answered her back, "Well, who begun it?"
That's what at the end of a war
We always say — not who won it,
Or what it was foughten for.

The Milky Way Is a Cowpath

On wings too stiff to flap
We started to exult
In having left the map
On journey the penult.

But since we got nowhere,
Like small boys we got mad
And let go at the air
With everything we had.

Incorrigible Quid-nuncs,
We *would* see what would come
Of pelting heaven with chunks
Of crude uranium.

At last in self-collapse
We owned up to our wife
The Milky Way perhaps
Was woman's way of life.

Our un-outwitted spouse
Replied she had as soon
Believe it was the cow's
That overshot the moon.

The parabolic curve
Of her celestial track

As any might observe
Might never bring her back.

The famous foster nurse
Of man and womankind
Had for the universe
Left trivia behind;

And gone right on astray
Through let-down pasture bars
Along the Milky Way
A-foraging on stars,

Perennial as flowers,
To where as some allege
This universe of ours
Has got a razor edge;

And if she don't take care
She'll get her gullet cut,
But that is no affair
Of anybody's but —

The author of these words
Whose lifelong unconcern
Has been with flocks and herds
For what they didn't earn.

Some Science Fiction

The chance is the remotest
Of its going much longer unnoticed
That I'm not keeping pace
With the headlong human race.

And some of them may mind
My staying back behind
To take life at a walk
In philosophic talk;

Though as yet they only smile
At how slow I do a mile,
With tolerant reproach
For me as an Old Slow Coach.

But I know them what they are:
As they get more nuclear
And more bigoted in reliance
On the gospel of modern science,

For them my loitering around
At less than the speed of sound
Or even the speed of light
Won't seem unheretical quite.

They may end by banishing me
To the penal colony

They are thinking of pretty soon
Establishing on the moon.

With a can of condensed air
I could go almost anywhere,
Or rather submit to be sent
As a noble experiment.

They should try one wastrel first
On a landscape so accursed
To see how long they should wait
Before they make it a state.

*

ENVOI TO HYDE THE CASTAWAY

OF CROW ISLAND

I made this you to beguile
With some optimism for Christmas
On your isle that would be an isle
But isn't because it's an isthmus.

QUANDARY

Quandary

Never have I been sad or glad
That there was such a thing as bad.
There had to be, I understood,
For there to have been any good.
It was by having been contrasted
That good and bad so long had lasted.
That's why discrimination reigns.
That's why we need a lot of brains
If only to discriminate
'Twixt what to love and what to hate.
To quote the oracle of Delphi,
Love thou thy neighbor as thyself, aye,
And hate him as thyself thou hatest.
There quandary is at its greatest.
We learned from the forbidden fruit
For brains there is no substitute.
"Unless it's sweetbreads," you suggest
With innuendo I detest.
You drive me to confess in ink:
Once I was fool enough to think
That brains and sweetbreads were the same,
Till I was caught and put to shame,
First by a butcher, then a cook,
Then by a scientific book.
But 'twas by making sweetbreads do
I passed with such a high I.Q.

A Reflex

Hear my rigmarole.
Science stuck a pole
Down a likely hole
And he got it bit.
Science gave a stab
And he got a grab.
That was what he got.
"Ah," he said, "Qui vive,
Who goes there, and what
ARE we to believe?
That there is an It?"

In a Glass of Cider

It seemed I was a mite of sediment
That waited for the bottom to ferment
So I could catch a bubble in ascent.
I rode up on one till the bubble burst
And when that left me to sink back reversed
I was no worse off than I was at first.
I'd catch another bubble if I waited.
The thing was to get now and then elated.

From Iron

TOOLS AND WEAPONS

To Ahmed S. Bokhari

Nature within her inmost self divides
To trouble men with having to take sides.

Four-room shack aspiring high
With an arm of scrawny mast
For the visions in the sky
That go blindly pouring past.
In the ear and in the eye
What you get is what to buy.
Hope you're satisfied to last.

But outer Space,
At least this far,
For all the fuss
Of the popul*ace*,
Stays more popul*ar*
Than popul*ous*.

On Being Chosen Poet of Vermont

Breathes there a bard who isn't moved
When he finds his verse is understood
And not entirely disapproved
By his country and his neighborhood?

We vainly wrestle with the blind belief
That aught we cherish
Can ever quite pass out of utter grief
And wholly perish.

It takes all sorts of in and outdoor schooling
To get adapted to my kind of fooling.

In winter in the woods alone
Against the trees I go.
I mark a maple for my own
And lay the maple low.

At four o'clock I shoulder axe
And in the afterglow
I link a line of shadowy tracks
Across the tinted snow.

I see for Nature no defeat
In one tree's overthrow
Or for myself in my retreat
For yet another blow.